Working With QuickBooks® Customers - Part 1

Version 2013

Dwayne J. Briscoe, President
http://www.bookkeeping-results.com

Introduction

Working and teaching hundreds of small business owners and bookkeepers throughout the years, I have learned that education is the key to success.

This material is for informational purposes only and is not intended to substitute for obtaining accounting, tax, or legal advice from a licensed professional for your particular situation. There is no liability or responsibility assumed for any errors or omissions in the content of this book, as federal and state laws and policies may change. The U.S. and Texas state tax advice contained in this book is not intended to be used for the purpose of avoiding penalties under federal or state law. Reasonable efforts have been made to furnish accurate and up-to-date information, however it is not warranted that it is accurate, complete, reliable, current, or error free. Information has been obtained from the Texas Workforce Commission, the Internal Revenue Service, the Social Security Administration, and the United States Department of Labor.

About the Author

Dwayne J. Briscoe is a Certified QuickBooks ProAdvisor® with over 10 years of experience supporting businesses and individuals who utilize QuickBooks®. Since Dwayne's work in teaching QuickBooks® for over 7 years, he has taught over 1,000 small business owners and bookkeepers through local area Small Business Development Centers,
public and private instruction, and Brazosport College.

Working With Your QuickBooks® Customers Part 1

Objective 1 - Learn how to create a customer list and review the different aspects of the information you add to the Customer.

Objective 2 - Learn how the Lead Center works and how to import the leads into the Customer Center.

Objective 3 - Working with customers who will utilize a sales tax exempt certificate or a resale tax exempt certificate.

Objective 4 - Work with jobs and sub jobs for your customers.

Objective 5 - Understanding the differences between: Estimates, Sales Orders, Invoices and Sales Receipts.

Objective 1 – Learn how to create a customer list and review the different aspects of the information you add to the Customer.

In QuickBooks, customers are who supply the company income, and jobs are specifically titled projects for which your customers may have more than one specific project for your goods and/or services that you want to maintain.

While going through the set-up of your information in the various Centers, you will see that QuickBooks® will automatically link pieces of information to prevent you from having to retype it. You also are not required to enter any information EXCEPT for the identifying Name. The extra information fields are optional pieces of resource material to maximize your information.

Each customer is a completely separate entry, so whatever information you add or don't add, will be related only to that particular customer or job you're working with. In the long-term the more information you have, the stronger your company's knowledge base.

No Customer, Vendor, and Employee can have the same name, so if you work with different people or companies in two or three of these Centers, you must show them differently. An example would be adding a hyphen, a period, or an asterisk at the end of one of the entries.

To reach the Customer Center, you have three options:

Option 1 – on the Home Page, you will move your cursor to the "Customers" label noted below:

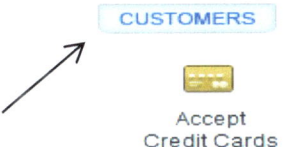

Accept
Credit Cards

Option 2 – on the Menu Bar, you will see the word Customers, and when you move your cursor over it, you choose the first drop-down item which is Customer Center.

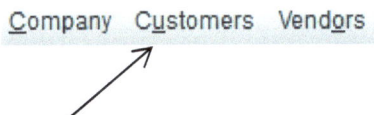

Option 3 – there are a number of short-cut keys, and typing Ctrl-J will take you directly to the Customer Center

The Customer Center

To add a new customer:

a. Choose the New Customer & Job button in the upper left corner, and then choose New Customer from the drop down list. From there you will see the blank Customer screen appear as shown below.

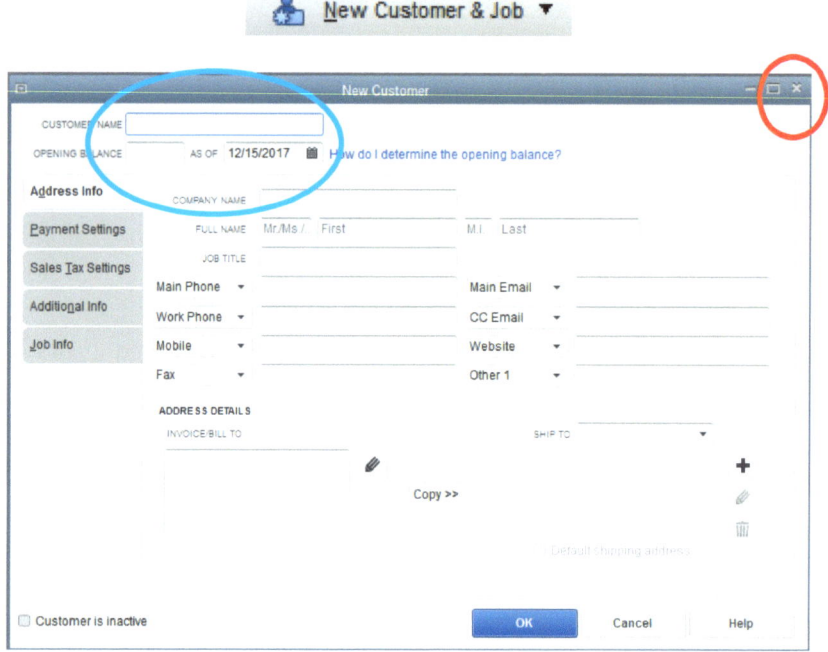

b. The "Opening Balance" field shows what is currently owed from the customer. Upon entering the outstanding invoices, this will be calculated from the Accounts Receivable account. The "As Of" date shows to when the outstanding balance was entered, but do not enter any amount in this box because it will skew the correct accounts receivable amount.

c. A new window will appear to input your customer information, however close out of the window by choosing the Cancel button. Next, in the upper right-hand corner of the screen, click on the "x" and that will close out the new customer.

d. Next, when your Customer Center is open again, highlight Kristy Abercrombie by using your cursor and then choose the Edit button for Kristy Abercrombie (located on the right-hand side of the screen that looks like a fork), which is what we'll be working with for the duration of this lesson.

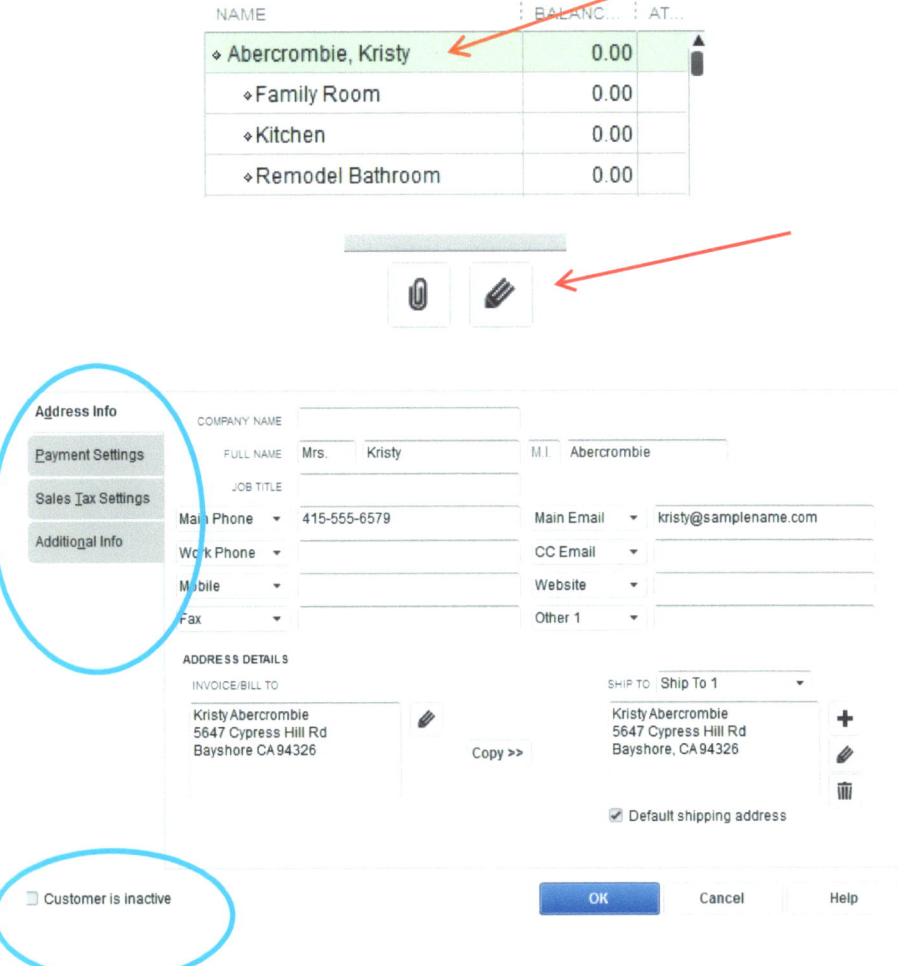

On the main page of each Customer, you will see four buttons on the left side of your screen: Address Info, Payment Settings, Sales Tax Settings, and Additional Information.

The "Customer Is Inactive" box in the bottom left side of the window will be unchecked. Its purpose is if you are no longer working with a customer it is still present in the file but no longer an option for you to choose unless you re-activate it. Although these customers are inactive, they cannot be deleted if they have any transactions attached, i.e. invoices, estimates, sales orders, etc.

Address Info tab

The first tab is labeled Address Info. When you view the drop-down menu from each of the Address Info windows, you can arrange and them as you choose in a variety of combinations and what is appearing currently is the default.

Note that hitting the TAB button will allow you to move through each field on the screen from top to bottom, and then left to right.

The "Customer Name" field is what will be identified in your Customer Center. If you are listing individuals, then determine if you want to list last name then first name, or first name then last name, which will show how the list is sorted. This will also help prevent potential duplications of customers.

Be sure that whatever process you choose, it is consistent throughout. If you are listing companies, the "Customer Name" and "Company Name" fields should be the same unless you want to list the "Company Name" as a parent company and the "Customer Name" as a subsidiary of the parent.

The "Company Name" field does not need to be completed if you are listing an individual as your customer. However if it is filled out, then it will automatically be typed into the "Bill To" field by QuickBooks® and placed underneath the "Company Name."

The "Mr./Mrs./Ms." salutation field is used if you are listing your contact individual. If you begin using this field identifying contacts, then it should be used with all of your customers, for consistency.

The "First Name / Initial / Last Name" fields should be completed if your correspondence is going to be directed towards a specific individual at a company or your customer is an individual. Once you enter the information in each field and hit TAB, it will automatically be typed into the "Bill To" field.

The Job Title allows you to specifically address the customer's work position.
The Main Phone, Work Phone, Mobile, Fax, Main Email, CC Email, Web Site, and Other 1 are additional default fields to complete for your contact's information. Please note that the drop-down for each of these fields allows you to change the order and list.

The "Invoice/Bill To" field shows where the invoices and statements are to be delivered to. Because you already have the Company and Contact Names typed in for you, you need to type in the street address or PO Box, City, State, Zip Code, and Country information if it is outside of your country. Because companies often have a mailing address different than their physical location, this will be addressed shortly.

If you click on the Edit button, you will see a checked box on the bottom of the screen that says "Show this window again when address is incomplete or unclear." The purpose of this button is to automatically appear if you should forget to put in the zip code, state abbreviation, etc. Unchecking the box will prevent the message from appearing again in the future, but it's best to leave checked to prevent the use of inaccurate information. You will also have the option of "Note" field to put in additional information such as mailing address only, etc.

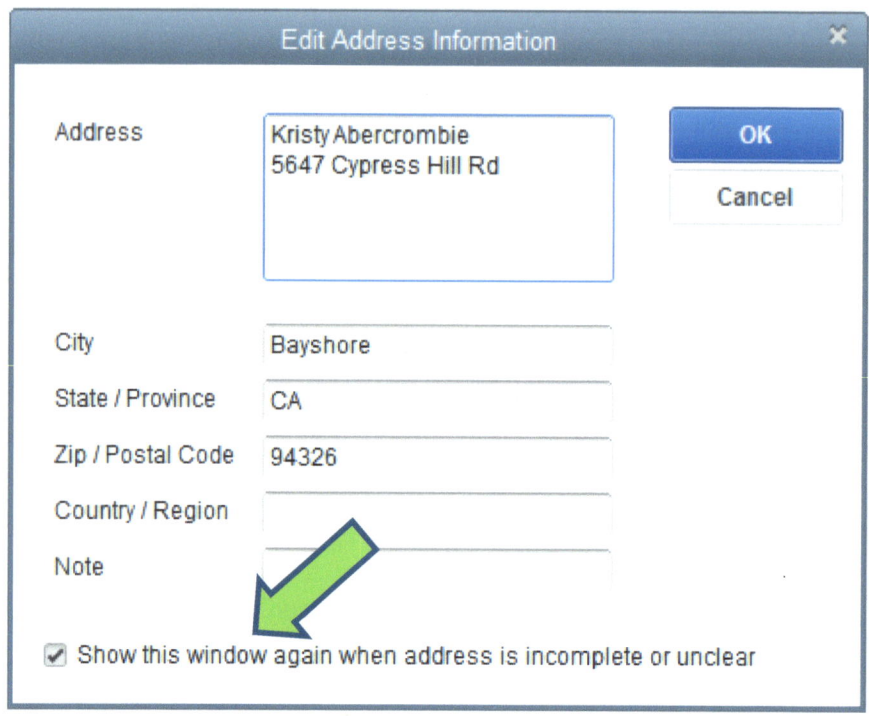

To demonstrate this, if you were to take out the Zip Code and then go back to re-entering the information, the message box that we just looked at will appear alerting us to the problem. It's the way to allow QuickBooks® to prevent you from printing anything without a complete address.

"Ship To" field gives the customer multiple locations by using the drop-down arrow where it says "Ship to 1" to have your products and/or services sent to an address different from the "Bill To" field. When you click on the drop down arrow and choose <Add New>, the "Address Name" will automatically say "Ship To 1" but can be changed to another title.

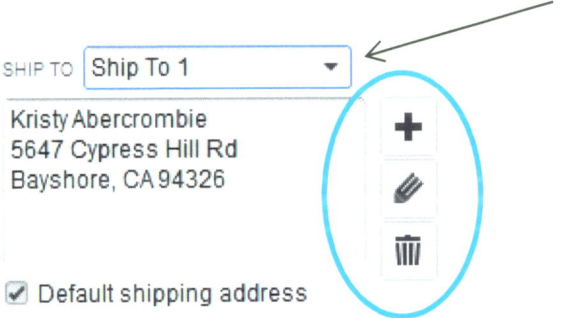

Just like in the "Bill To" field, it will require you to type in the street address / PO Box, City, State, Zip Code, and Country information if it is outside of your country. This is where you are able to list your customer's physical address if they have a separate mailing address. Since our Customer may have PO Box for their correspondence, we're going to use this field as their main address.

The ✚ symbol allows you to automatically add a new shipping address.

The ✐ symbol allows you to edit the currently open shipping address.

The 🗑 symbol allows you delete the currently open shipping address.

Payment Settings Tab

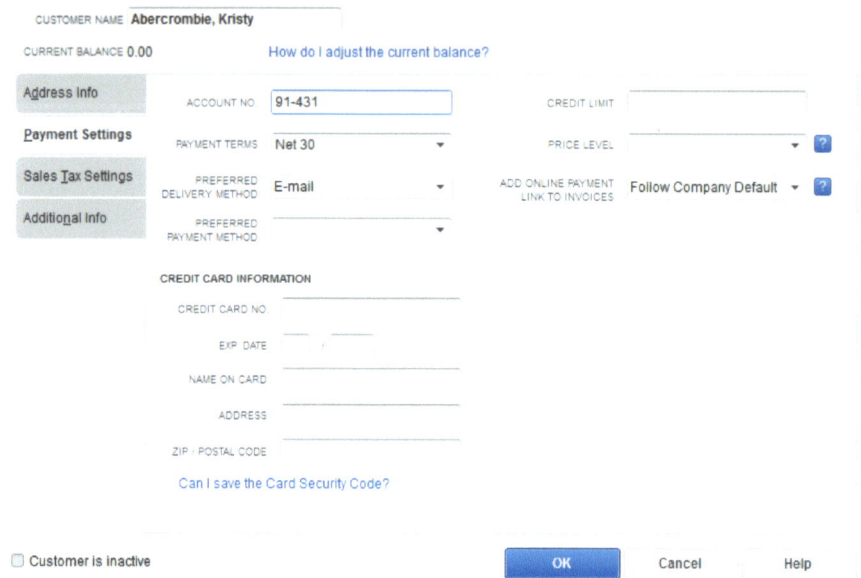

"Account No." refers to what customer number you may assign to the customer. QuickBooks does not do any assigning. If you choose not to assign one, then you leave it blank.

"Payment Terms" field determines the length of time your customers have to pay their invoices. If you choose no terms on a customer, then it will automatically be considered "Due on receipt" when QuickBooks prints the date on your invoice.

Be aware that if you choose the "1% 10 Net 30" or "2% 10 Net 30," you are giving terms that will allow your customers to take a 1% or 2% discount respectively by paying within the first 10 days of the date of the invoice or the total amount within 30 days. For our customer, we're going to choose "Net 15."

If you choose to add a new term, when you use the drop-down arrow you will see the "Add New" option, and the following window will appear and allow you to develop your own set of payment terms for your customers.

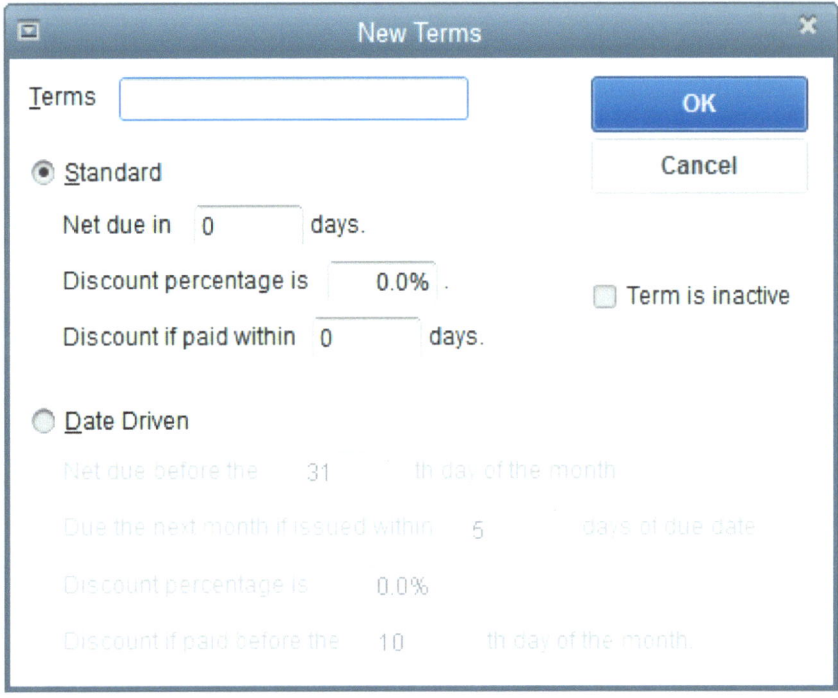

The "Standard" option asks within how many days the bill should be due, if you want to offer a discount percentage amount, and if so how many days before the discount option will expire. When using these terms, make sure anyone entering new customers is aware of how they work.

⦿ Date Driven
Net due before the   31   th day of the month.

Due the next month if issued within   5   days of due date.

Discount percentage is   0.0% .

Discount if paid before the   10   th day of the month.

The "Date Driven" option asks what day of the month the invoice will be due, if you choose a particular day of the month such as the default 31st but the invoice is within 5 days of it such as the 29th, then it will be changed to the following month's 31st day as to when the bill is due.

The discount percentage is also available, but if you use it you must calculate how many days from your day of the month the invoice will be due. An example is if you choose the bill is due on the 31st and you send it out on March 29th, QuickBooks® will change the due date to April 30th because of the 5 day rule.

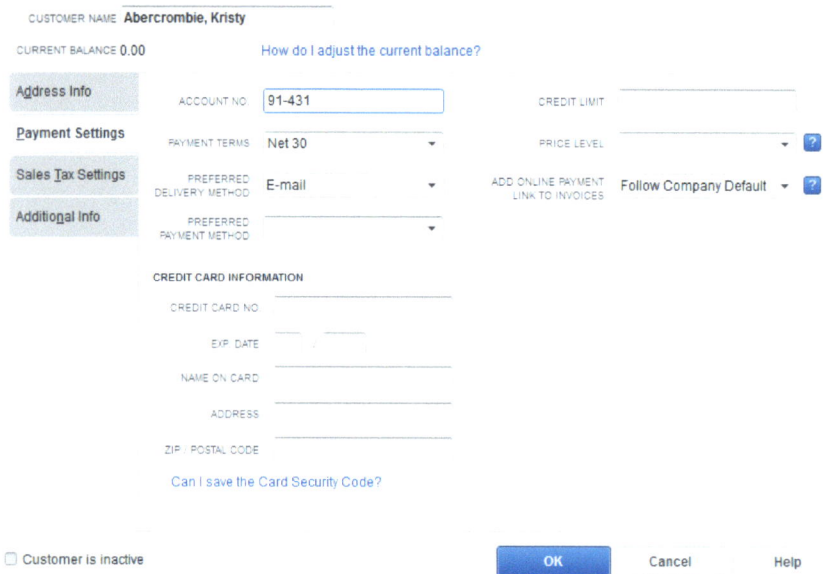

"Preferred Delivery Method" field allows you to choose either "Mail," "E-mail," or "None." If you choose "E-mail," then you must have a valid e-mail address on the "Address Info" tab and in the Company information section. If you choose "Mail," then it will automatically default your customer-related invoices, statements, sales orders, and estimates set to print. If you choose "None," you will have to manually either e-mail or print each item. For our customer, we're going to choose "E-mail."

"Preferred Payment Method" section allows you to keep track of how your customers make their payments, through:

Cash / Check / American Express / Discover / MasterCard / Visa / Barter / E-Check

This section is ideal for credit card users who don't want to always reveal their information each time they make payments. For this option you need to type in:
- Credit Card No.
- Exp. Date
- Name on Card
- Address
- Zip Code

Be aware that the Security Card Code that some businesses required (the last three digits on the back of MasterCard, VISA and Discover, or the four digits on the front of American Express) cannot be saved because it violates the Payment Applications Best Practices guidelines for handling credit card information handed down by the Payment Card Industry for software providers.

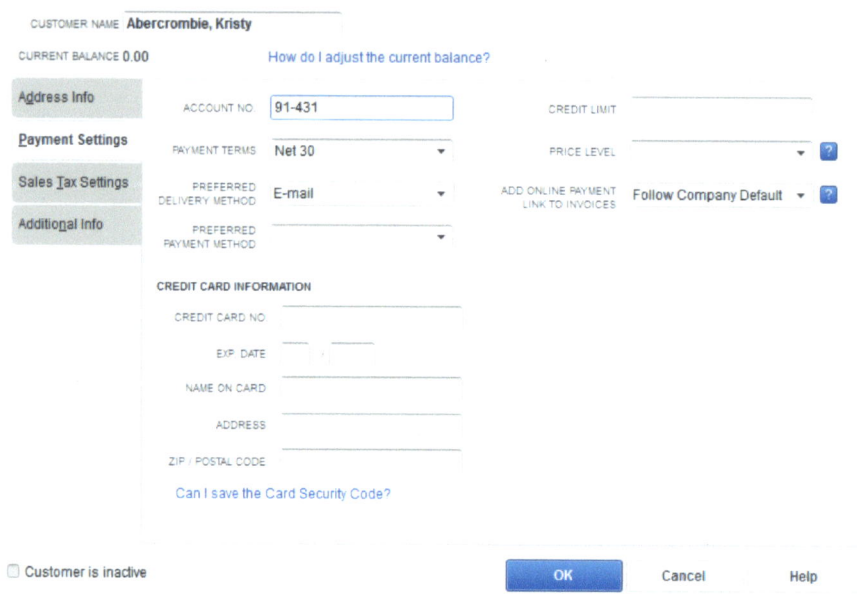

If your business requires it, you will need to request this information each time. If you process credit cards through QuickBooks® Merchant Services or use the Online payment link to invoices, saving this information can automatically be used in the "Receive Payments" section so you don't retype it when processing payments.

"Credit Limit" field refers to the amount of credit you extend to your customers. If a customer exceeds the limit placed in this field when preparing a new invoice, then a warning will appear before you save the customer's invoice alerting you to the issue. The sales person processing the invoice and receiving this warning has the choice of either overriding or cancelling the invoice.

"Price Level" field refers to specific price increases and/or discounts that you offer your customers. You can either set your price on a per-item or a percentage discount based on different customers or jobs. If you choose "Per Item," you must name the pricing structure and then set prices for the customer, which can be used for other customers. If you choose "Fixed Percentage," you have the options of increasing or decreasing the percentage by the amount you choose and then allow you to perform customized rounding.

This pricing applies to only billable time and mileage; however it's not automatic for any items or expenses that are from your own purchases or from invoices that are created from an Estimate.

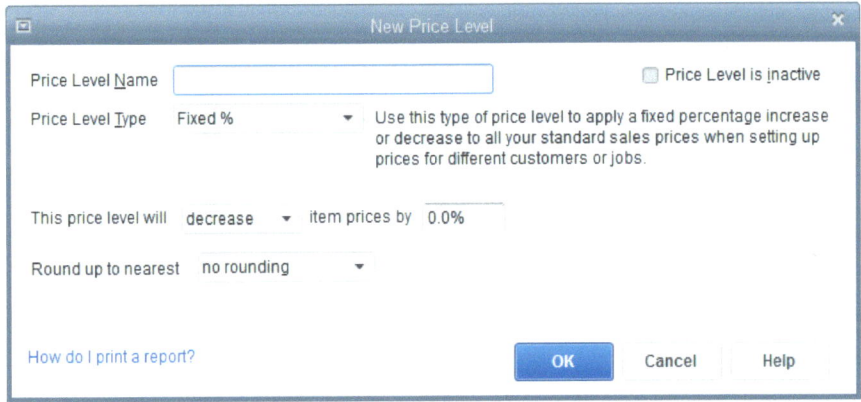

For each Price Level if you are using the fixed percentage you will either increase or decrease the item price by a certain percentage amount, and then determine how you will handle the rounding.

For each Price Level if you are using the Per Item option, each item that is set up in your Items List will be what you choose to be affected or not affected. Once you set this up one time, you will not need to set it up for other Customers – you go into each Customer that is affected and choose each Price Level that is applied.

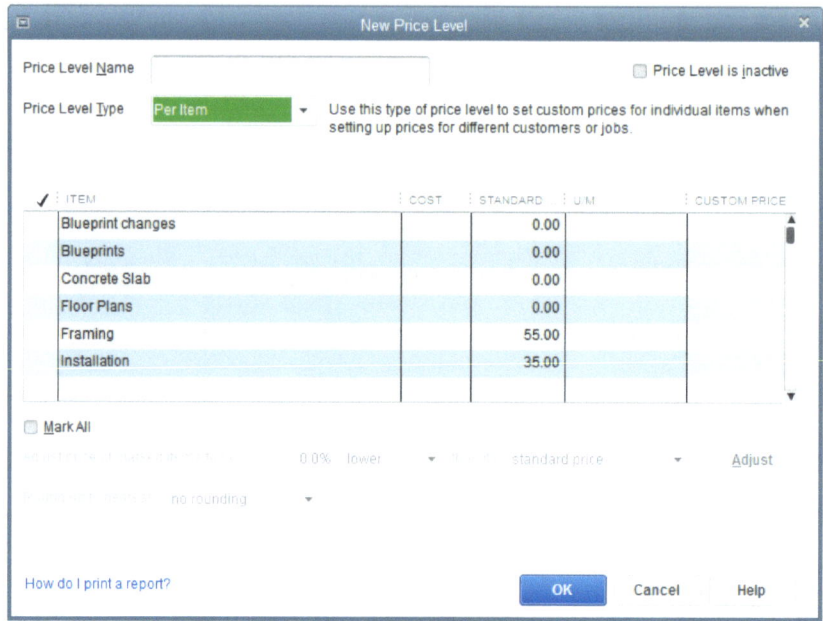

"Add Online Payment Link to Invoices" as described in the Edit / Preferences / Administrator / Payments section allows you to choose individually what Customers you want to offer this option and what Customers you do not.

Sales Tax Settings Tab

If you are not required to charge sales tax for any products or services to any customers, you will need to change the Tax Code to "Non" from the drop-down menu of the Tax Code.

If you are required to charge sales tax, then we will go step-by-step through the rest of the section. If you have ANY questions about whether or not you should be charging sales tax on the products and/or services you sell, contact your State Comptroller or Revenue Department office to prevent any potential customers not taxed properly.

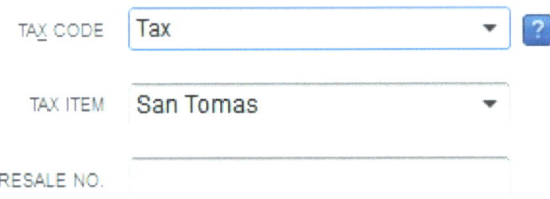

"Tax Code" field designates whether the customer is charged sales tax, for which you will choose "Tax."

"Tax Item" field refers to what tax the customer is charged. If you have multiple tax entities, this is where you will need to choose which one is collected for your customer. An example is service personnel who make on-site calls in various tax jurisdictions which have different city/county rates in addition to the state sales tax rate.

"Resale No." field refers to customers that are exempt from sales tax.

Additional Info Tab

"Customer Type" field will initially list such identifiers as Commercial and Residential. The purpose of "Type" is used if you are tracking how your customers found your business. If you want to add new types, click on the drop down arrow, click on <Add New>, then add in your new type.

Examples could be: mail out lists, on-line, internet, etc. For our customer, we're going to add Internet. When we select "Add New" we're going to type in "Internet Advertisement" and then check the Subtype box and choose Residential.

Click OK to save the new Customer Type. This allows you to know that you have a residential customer who found you through an internet advertisement, to help determine at a later date if you should continue promoting through the internet or not when you are reviewing your marketing expenses.

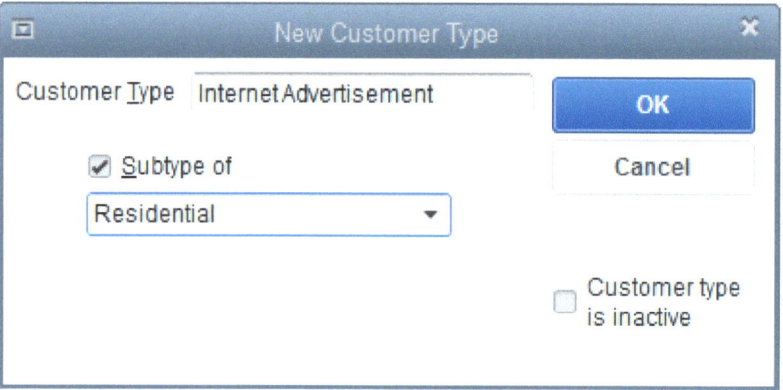

Custom Fields

"Custom Fields" section allows you to define up to seven individual fields for further tracking of your information. This section is also found in the Vendor and Employee Centers. When you click on "Define Fields" you will see a variety of blank label fields with blank boxes to be checked for each of the Centers.

You can have up to 7 fields available in all three centers, two centers, or just one center. Items such as birthday, spouse name, etc. are examples to be used in this section. These can be added and deleted at any time.

CUSTOM FIELDS

CONTRACT #

B-DAY   1/1/65

SPOUSE'S NAME   Tim

Define Fields

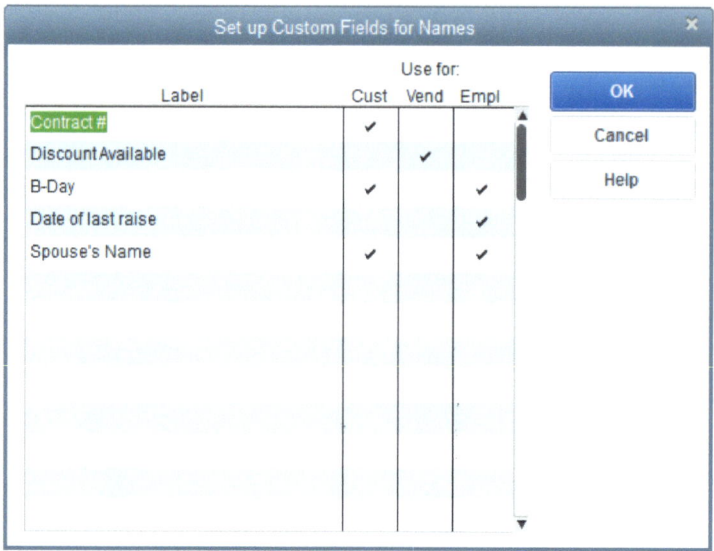

Customer Information Section

When you enter all of the information, as shown in the sample company file, you will see all of the pertinent information that has been entered. If you need to go back and edit that customer's information, you will see what looks like a three-pronged tool, which allows you to go back into the Customer Information section.

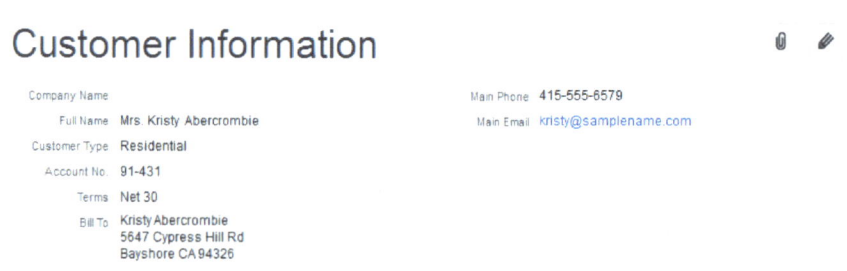

The Transactions tab shows everything between the Company and the Customer.

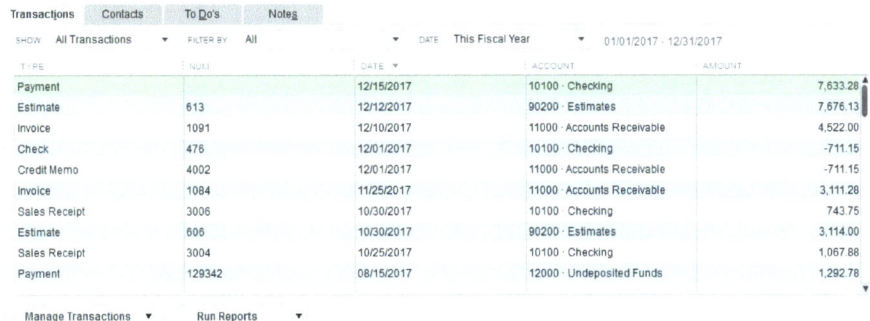

The Contacts tab shows the people associated with this Customer who you interact with.

The To Do's allows you the opportunity to add various tasks, i.e. Call, Fax, E-Mail, Meeting, Appointment, and Task.

When you want to add a To Do item, choose the "Manage To Do's" drop-down menu at the bottom left-hand side of the window and select Create New. The Run Reports drop-down menu allows you to see what you have/have not accomplished.

The following pop-up window will allow you to choose the Type of task you want to set as a reminder and what the Priority is (Low, Medium, or High). When choosing the "With" option, you have the opportunity to set the task for a Customer, Vendor, Employee, or Lead. If you want set only a date, change the Due date to when it's necessary.

If you want to specify a time, make sure that the box is checked to allow you to set the appropriate time for your To Do task to appear. The Details section allows you to put all necessary information to inform you of the task that you need to complete. The Status drop-down menu allows you to either leave the task Active, Done, or Inactive.

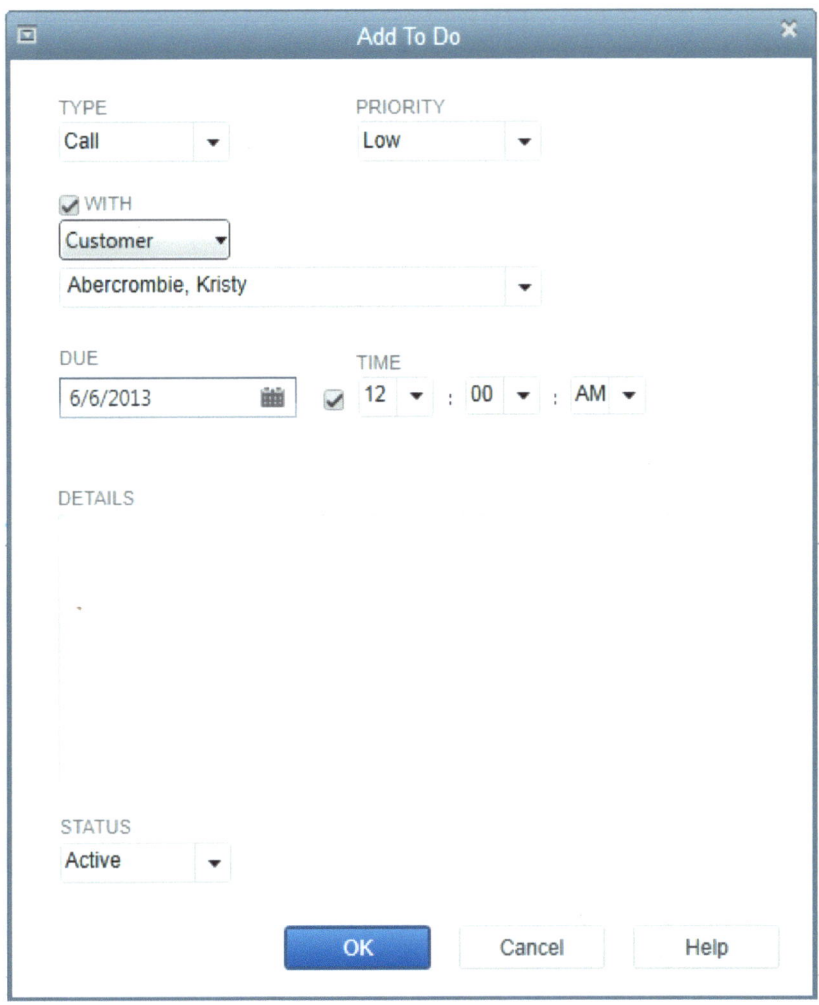

The Notes section allows you to write all of your documentation information as it's necessary for that customer. To add notes, choose the Manage Notes drop-down menu to either: Add New, Edit Selected Note, or Delete Selected Note. All of the notes for the Customer will appear on the right-hand side of the Notes section.

When you add a new Note, your customer's previous contact information is available as a reference. The Date/Time Stamp button allows you to pinpoint the moment you wrote the note. The New To Do... button allows you to add a new task, as described above. The Print button allows all of the notes to be printed as a hard copy.

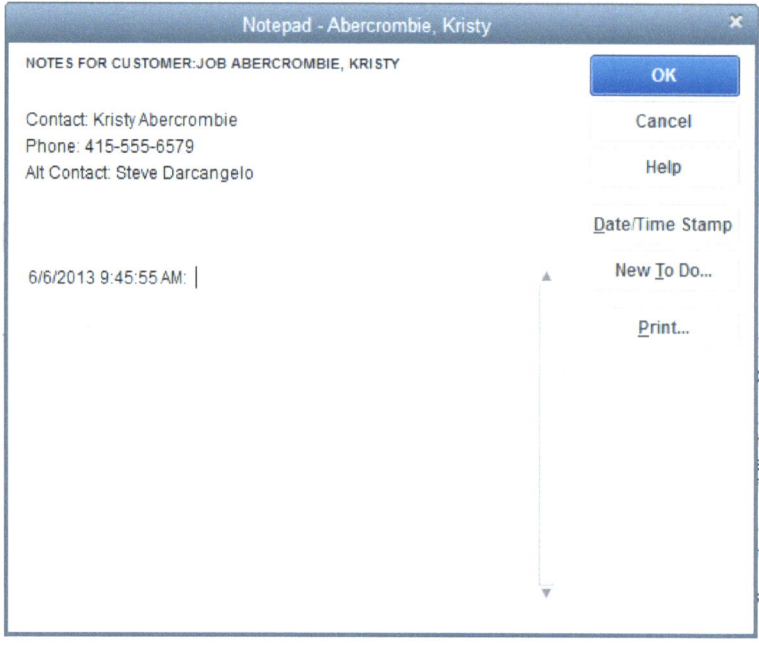

Exercises

1.   The short-cut key to present the Customer Center is:

_____

2.   What is the first tab that opens when you add a new Customer: _____

3.   A Customer, Vendor, and/or Employee have the same name?

      a. True
      b. False

4.   How many tabs are available to add information to a Customer?

      a. 1
      b. 2
      c. 3
      d. 4

5.   You can use a fixed percentage rate when setting price levels.

      a. True
      b. False

6.   2% 10 Net 30 refers to giving a customer a 2% discount when they pay within how many days?

_____

7.   The Security Card Code can be kept on file with a customer's credit card information.

      a. True
      b. False

Objective 2 – Learn how the Lead Center works and how to import the leads into the Customer Center.

The Lead Center allows QuickBooks users to track their prospects and import them into the Customer Center. To open the Lead Center, choose the drop-down menu from either the Company or Customers from the Menu Bar.

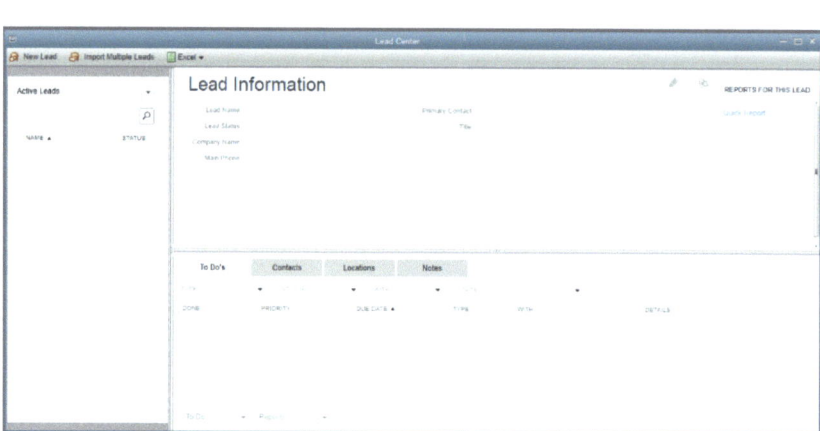

You have two options of adding prospects to the Lead Center. You can add a New Lead individually, import Multiple Leads from Excel, and the Excel drop-down menu allows you to export reports from your Lead Center.

New Lead

When you choose New Lead, you will need to at least complete the Name field with information.

The Status drop-down menu offers you the opportunity of stating if the lead is Hot, Warm, or Cold for tracking purposes. The Company information allows you to input as much information as possible in order to centralize your resources.

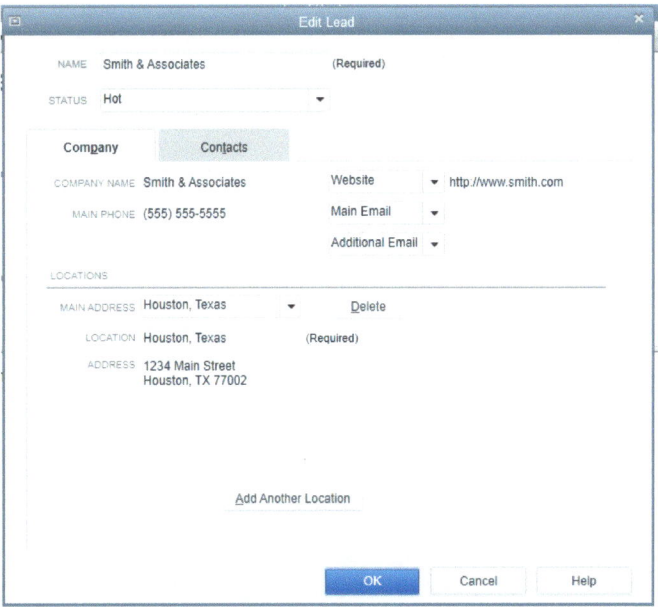

The Contacts section allows you to add multiple contacts with that particular company. Unlike the Customer Center, when you add information to the Contacts, you must re-enter each line as it is not transferred automatically.

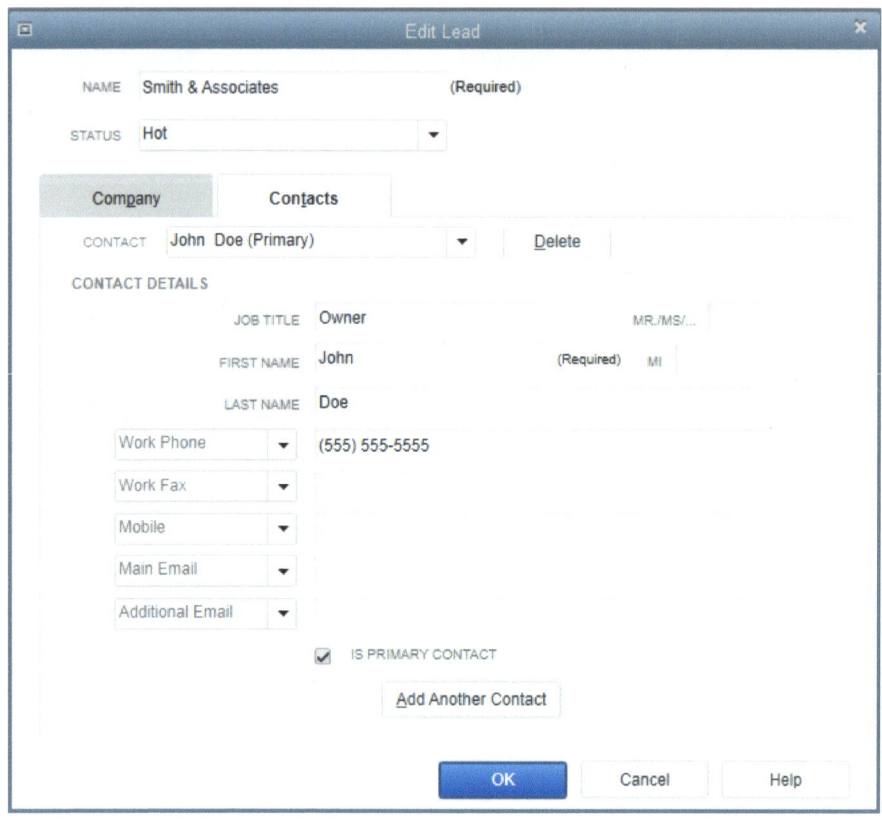

When you complete the information for each lead, its appearance is similar to the Customer's profile section. The difference is that you will see a different icon on the top right side of the menu next to "Reports For This Lead" which when you choose, can import this Lead as a Customer.

Underneath the Lead Information window, you will have the same options as you would in the Customer Center. Any information that you have inputed into the Lead will be transferred into the Customer's information.

Import Multiple Leads

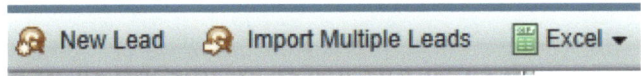

You can enter Multiple Leads either by manually entering them or importing them from Excel by the cut and paste method. At the bottom left hand corner of the window, you will see "0 Leads inserted" and it will keep count as to how many leads that you import.

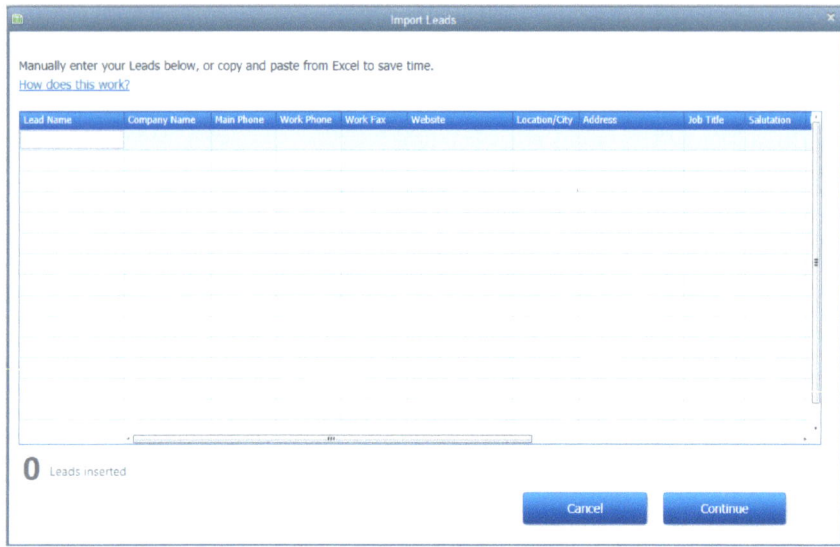

When you are pasting information from an Excel spreadsheet into this window, follow these instructions:

 a. after you open your spreadsheet, copy each column that you are entering by using Ctrl+C
 b. for each column you've copied, move your cursor to the first field for each column where you're doing the pasting and then choose Ctrl+V in order to paste the information
 c. upon completing the copy and paste procedure, click Continue and then complete the importation

Excel Option

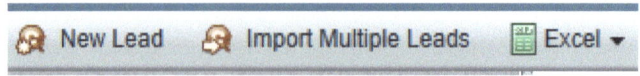

The Excel drop-down menu allows you to export the following reports into Excel:

 - Lead Contact List
 - Lead Status List
 - Converted Leads

Exercises

1.   You can cut and paste your leads from what Microsoft Office software?

_____

2.   You need to retype the information when a Lead becomes a Customer.

        a. True
        b. False

Objective 3 - Working with customers who utilize a sales tax exempt certificate or a resale tax exempt certificate.

If you have a state that charges sales tax, then you should contact your State Comptroller or Department of Revenue. In this example, per the laws of the State of Texas, if the customer is recognized as a nonprofit organization, they must receive a written approval letter from the state, not from the federal government or IRS Office, and will be given an identification number for their exemption. They must then provide you a Texas Sales and Use Exemption Certificate which will give their contact information, their identification number, note the goods and/or services sold to them, and signed by an authorized representative.

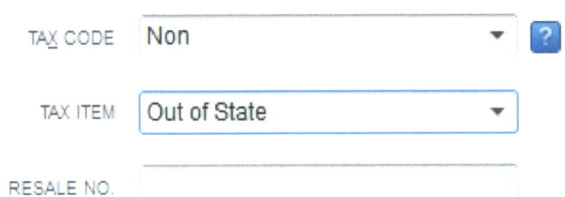

Customers may also require you to collect the appropriate sales tax on their behalf to avoid the process of reporting and payments from their own accounting departments, which is another avenue of responsibility when working with the sales tax field.

The Resale No." field refers to their sales tax exempt number from one of two certificates. The first certificate is that the customer is recognized as a 501(c)3 organization and exempt from sales tax by its state. They must receive a written approval letter from the state and will be given an identification number for their exemption. They must then provide you a Sales and Use Exemption Certificate which will give their contact information, their identification number, note the goods and/or services sold to them, and signed by an authorized representative.

If you want to verify an organization's Texas sales tax exempt status and what items/services are exempt, you can use the link below and the following search window will appear:

http://window.state.tx.us/taxinfo/exempt/exempt_search.html

Other states will have similar verifiable databases through their Comptroller or Department of Revenue sites.

Texas Tax-Exempt Entity Search

Search and obtain online verification of nonprofit and other types of organizations that hold state tax exemption from:

- Sales and Use Tax
- Franchise Tax
- Hotel Occupancy Tax

Statewide group organizations might have one listing with "All Branches" as the city, rather than a separate listing for each local chapter. Search by:

1. Taxpayer Number OR
2. Organization Name/City/County

Taxpayer Number Search ——————————————————————————————

Enter 11-digit Taxpayer Number

Organization Name/City/County Search ——————————————————————

Organization Name

Organization Name search can be narrowed by combining this search with a city or county name below.

City

Searching by city name only will return a listing of all exempt organizations in that city.

County

Searching by county name only will return a listing of all exempt organizations in that county. This search includes Texas counties only.

Submit   Reset

Texas Sales and Use Tax Resale Certificate

Name of purchaser, firm or agency as shown on permit	Phone (Area code and number)
Address (Street & number, P. O. Box or Route number)	
City, State, ZIP code	
Texas Sales and Use Tax Permit Number (must contain 11 digits)	
Out-of-state retailer's registration number or Federal Taxpayers Registry (RFC) number for retailers based in Mexico	
	(Retailers based in Mexico must also provide a copy of their Mexico registration form to the seller.)

I, the purchaser named above, claim the right to make a non-taxable purchase (for resale of the taxable items described below or on the attached order or invoice) from:

Seller: _____

Street address: _____

City, State, ZIP code: _____

Description of items to be purchased on the attached order or invoice:

_____

_____

_____

Description of the type of business activity generally engaged in or type of items normally sold by the purchaser:

_____

_____

The taxable items described above, or on the attached order or invoice, will be resold, rented or leased by me within the geographical limits of the United States of America, its territories and possessions or within the geographical limits of the United Mexican States, in their present form or attached to other taxable items to be sold.

I understand that if I make any use of the items other than retention, demonstration or display while holding them for sale, lease or rental, I must pay sales tax on the items at the time of use based upon either the purchase price or the fair market rental value for the period of time used.

I understand that it is a criminal offense to give a resale certificate to the seller for taxable items that I know, at the time of purchase, are purchased for use rather than for the purpose of resale, lease or rental, and depending on the amount of tax evaded, the offense may range from a Class C misdemeanor to a felony of the second degree.

sign here ►	Purchaser	Title	Date

In Texas, this Resale Certificate is for the customer who is recognized as a reseller of the product you are selling them, for which they will use to resell to their customers. They must provide their contact information, their sales tax identification number, note the goods and/or services sold to them, and signed by an authorized representative. You must keep a copy of these certificates on file in the event you should be audited by the state comptroller's office. Failure to produce this paperwork upon request could cause significant fines and penalties for your business.

Texas Sales and Use Tax Exemption Certification
This certificate does not require a number to be valid.

SAVE A COPY	CLEAR SIDE

Name of purchaser, firm or agency	
Address (Street & number, P.O. Box or Route number)	Phone (Area code and number)
City, State, ZIP code	

I, the purchaser named above, claim an exemption from payment of sales and use taxes (for the purchase of taxable items described below or on the attached order or invoice) from:

Seller: _____

Street address: _____ City, State, ZIP code: _____

Description of items to be purchased or on the attached order or invoice:

_____

_____

_____

Purchaser claims this exemption for the following reason:

_____

_____

_____

I understand that I will be liable for payment of all state and local sales or use taxes which may become due for failure to comply with the provisions of the Tax Code and/or all applicable law.

I understand that it is a criminal offense to give an exemption certificate to the seller for taxable items that I know, at the time of purchase, will be used in a manner other than that expressed in this certificate, and depending on the amount of tax evaded, the offense may range from a Class C misdemeanor to a felony of the second degree.

sign here ▶	Purchaser	Title	Date

NOTE: This certificate cannot be issued for the purchase, lease, or rental of a motor vehicle.

THIS CERTIFICATE DOES NOT REQUIRE A NUMBER TO BE VALID.

Sales and Use Tax "Exemption Numbers" or "Tax Exempt" Numbers do not exist.

In Texas, this Exemption Certificate is for the customer who is recognized as being exempt from paying state sales tax. They must provide you their contact information, their identification number, note the goods and/or services sold to them, and signed by an authorized representative. It is important to keep a copy of these certificates on file in the event you should be audited by your state comptroller's office. Failure to produce this paperwork upon request could cause significant fines and penalties for your business.

You can use the link below to obtain copies of the pdf fillable forms for your Texas customers:

http://www.window.state.tx.us/taxinfo/taxforms/01-339.pdf

Setting Up Sales Tax Item(s)

When setting up the Sales Tax Item(s) in your Items List, you must set up the Sales Tax Tab in your Company Preferences under the Edit drop-down menu. If you are unsure if you should be charging sales tax, check with your State Comptroller or Revenue Department. In setting up the Sales Tax Item, you will be required to develop the most common sales tax item, which in this example we will use "Texas State."

When you go into Edit > Preferences > Sales Tax, the following window opens. You must be in the Company Preferences section in order to make changes to your Sales Tax options and go to the Company Preferences tab.

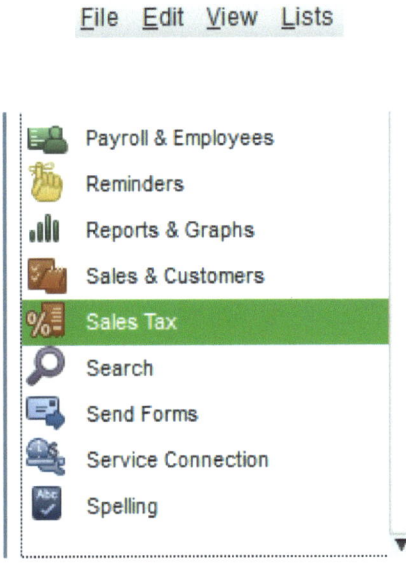

1. If you charge sales tax, you must choose Yes. If you do not then choose No.

My Preferences   Company Preferences

Do you charge sales tax?   ● Yes   ○ No

SET UP SALES TAX ITEM

Add a sales tax item for each county, district, parish, etc. where you collect sales tax.   Show Examples

Your most common sales tax item

Add sales tax item... | Texas State ▾

ASSIGN SALES TAX CODES

Sales tax codes determine if the items you sell are taxable or non-taxable.

Taxable item code   Tax ▾   Non-taxable item code   Non ▾

☑ Identify taxable amounts as "T" for "Taxable" when printing

WHEN DO YOU OWE SALES TAX?

○ As of invoice date (Accrual Basis)
● Upon receipt of payment (Cash Basis)

WHEN DO YOU PAY SALES TAX?

● Monthly
○ Quarterly
○ Annually

---

2. When completing the "Assign Tax Codes" you will default to what appears in the example above.

3. "When do you owe sales tax" is determined by whether or not you file your taxes on a cash or accrual basis.

4. "When do you pay sales tax" is determined by the schedule after receiving your sales tax permit from your State Comptroller."

5. When you choose "Add Sales Tax Item" the following window appears. From there you must choose "Sales Tax Item" for your "Type."

6. You type your "Sales Tax Name" which will be the governmental entity you are responsible to pay, which is limited to 14 characters.

7. You type your "Description," which will be much more detailed than your "Sales Tax Name."

8. You type your "Tax Rate" for the governmental entity you are responsible to pay.

9. You type the "Tax Agency" that is responsible for collecting your sales tax.

When you select Sales Tax Item, it will ask you for the Sales Tax Name, and the tax rate you are for your product or service. If you are located in a brick & mortar single location where you sell taxable items and services only at that location, you utilize one sales tax amount for its location.

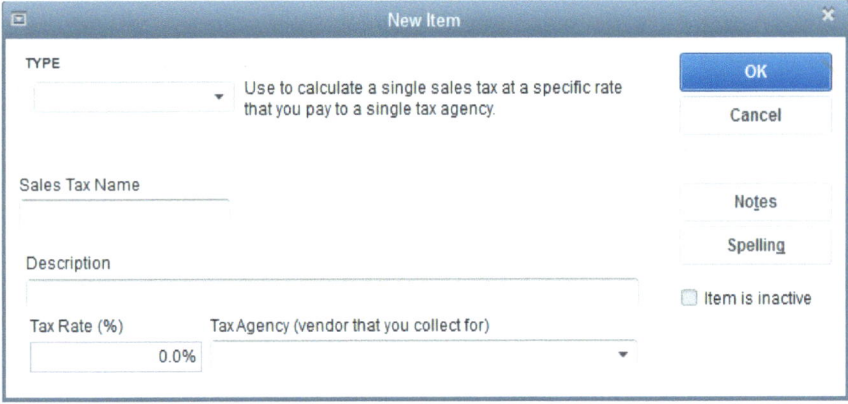

If you sell in multiple locations or perform taxable services in different locations, you must set up a different Sales Tax Item for each location based upon the area's physical location. In Texas, this is the link to find those multiple locations.

https://ourcpa.cpa.state.tx.us/atj/addresslookup.jsp

In the example below, we typed in State of Texas for the Name, "Sales Tax" will automatically be defaulted in the Description and "State of Texas" was added, the state rate of 6.25%, and then the governmental entity responsible for collections is the Texas State Comptroller.

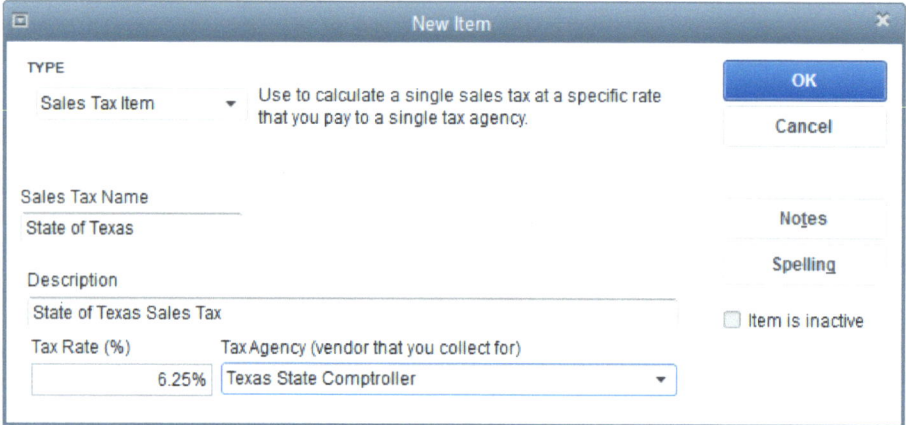

Because "Texas State Comptroller" was not already set up in the Vendor List, the following window will appear and ask you to either choose "Quick Add" which ONLY adds the name. If you choose "Set Up" then you can enter the full information, such as address, telephone number, etc. and then "Cancel" will not record any information.

The "Notes" and the "Spelling" options on the right side of the New Item window allows you to add additional notes to this particular item, as well as check the spelling for what you've typed. You also have the option of making the Item inactive.

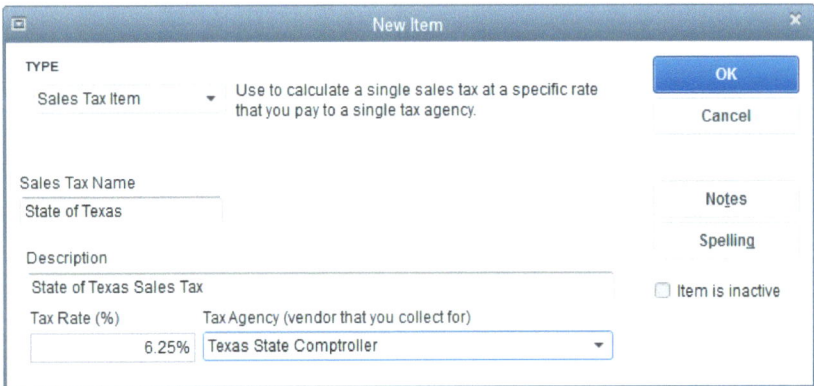

Because virtually every physical location in the United States has multiple tax entities, you must therefore assign each entity its own tax rate and set up a separate taxable item. From the taxable items, you will then develop a Sales Tax Item Group.

In the example below, it was noted that for 500 College Drive, Lake Jackson, Texas, there are three separate governmental entities for which sales tax must be collected. They are County, City, and State.

As of **January 30, 2013**, the following sales and use taxes apply at

500 COLLEGE DR
LAKE JACKSON, TX 77566-3136

The tax rate displayed is the tax rate for the address above and is valid for the current quarter only.

Jurisdiction Name	Local Code	Jurisdiction Type	Tax Rate
BRAZORIA	4020006	COUNTY	0.0050000
CLUTE	2020104	CITY	0.0150000
STATE SALES TAX		STATE	0.0625000
		Total Tax Rate:	**0.0825000**

As the State Tax Item has already been set up, you will use the same procedures for the County and City Tax Items. The Texas State Comptroller's Office collects and distributes all sales tax monies, they will also be listed as the default Tax Agency. It is important to make sure that all entities are listed and set-up properly in QuickBooks in the event of a sales tax audit and your file is requested as part of that process.

TYPE

Sales Tax Item   ▾   Use to calculate a single sales tax at a specific rate that you pay to a single tax agency.

Sales Tax Name

Brazoria

Description

Brazoria Sales Tax

Tax Rate (%)	Tax Agency (vendor that you collect for)
0.5%	Texas State Comptroller ▾

TYPE

Sales Tax Item   ▾   Use to calculate a single sales tax at a specific rate that you pay to a single tax agency.

Sales Tax Name

Clute

Description

Clute Sales Tax

Tax Rate (%)	Tax Agency (vendor that you collect for)
1.5%	Texas State Comptroller ▾

When you have completed all three jurisdictions, you will complete it with a Sales Tax Group. This gives you the total state tax payable of 8.25% (the maximum allowable by law in Texas) if your physical location is 500 College Drive. If you perform sales taxable services or sell your products at various locations, such as craft fairs or flea markets, trade shows, you must set up a similar Tax Group for each location. Each state has a maximum amount of sales tax it collects, so you must make sure that you are not collecting more than the maximum.

Setting Up Sales Tax Groups

In the same Sales Tax section of your Edit > Preferences, choose Sales Tax Group.

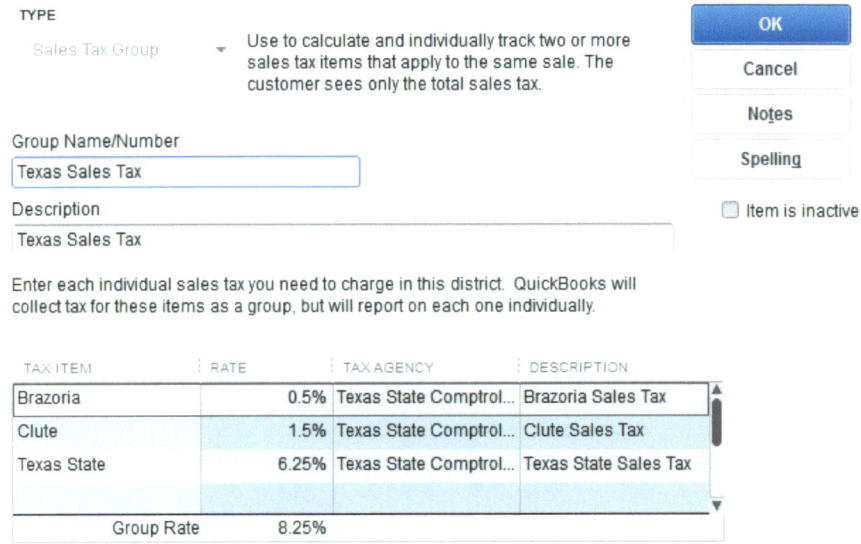

1. Group Name/Number – "Texas Sales Tax" informing you this is the tax collection for the state and includes the entities for your brick/mortar location of 500 College Drive, and it is limited to 22 characters.

2. Description – "Texas Sales Tax" can be the same as your Group Name/Number unless it needs to be longer than the 22 characters available.

3. Tax Item –Move your cursor into each non-shaded line under the Tax Item column, and from the drop down menu you will choose all 3 Sales Tax Items that you created, Brazoria, Clute, and Texas State. You will not be able to change the Rates, Tax Agency, or Description unless you go into the Item directly.

   If you do need to change the Sales Tax Item before or after you've created your Sales Tax Group, on your Menu Bar, you will need to choose List > Item List > find the Sales Tax Item > right click on your mouse while the Item is highlighted > edit the Sales Tax Item > Save & Close. If you need to edit your Sales Tax Group, following the same directions but highlight the Sales Tax Group instead and edit as needed.

Sales Tax in Multiple Areas

If you provide services and/or products in multiple areas, you may be responsible for collecting sales tax at that location for which the sale occurs. You must verify with your particular state comptroller's office in order to make sure that you are legally within compliance.

As an example, if your business is repairing air conditioning units, you must charge the appropriate sales tax based upon the address for the location and set up its own Sales Tax Group.

Below is a link to Avalara, a company which specializes in sales tax set-up and collection, which allows you to sign up for free look up of sales tax rates across the United States.

http://www.avalara.com/avaratesnow/avarateregistration

Sales Tax Out-of-State

As reported by the Sales Tax Institute, "You collect the tax for the state where the property is delivered to your customer. If the item is shipped to the customer, then tax applies for the delivery state. If the customer picks up the item at your location, tax should be collected for your state." Currently there are give states without general sales tax, which are: Alaska, Delaware, Montana, New Hampshire, and Oregon."

With current legislation related to internet sales tax, as well as states enacting their own collection procedures for received product shipments, it is important to review current and impending practices which may affect your business.

Exercises

1.   You often have the chance to pay your sales tax bi-annually.

   a. True
   b. False

2.   The sales tax rate is determined by knowing the following items except:

   a. Street Address
   b. County
   c. City
   d. Voting Precinct

3.   When you pay your sales tax on a cash or accrual basis, they are not based on any rules.

   a. True
   b. False

4.   When working with tax exempt organizations a 501(c)3 letter from the IRS sufficient to not charge state sales tax.

   a. True
   b. False

5.   The Resale No. refers to:

   a. the buyer's account #
   b. the seller's account #
   c. the buyer's sales tax permit #
   d. the seller's sales tax permit #

6.   You must set up your sales tax items before setting up your Sales Tax Groups.

   a. True
   b. False

7.   Sales tax rates on service sales are determined by where the action takes place.

   a. True
   b. False

Objective 4 - Work with jobs and sub jobs for your customers.

When you're working with a customer and you need to track several different tasks/jobs, it's important to consider adding jobs/sub jobs for each one. This allows you and your customer to track the progress and costs associated with a particular project.

NAME	BALANCE TOT...	ATTACH
⬦ Abercrombie, Kristy	0.00	
⬦ Family Room	0.00	
⬦ Kitchen	0.00	
⬦ Remodel Bathr...	0.00	

When it comes to developing a "Job Name," you want to make sure that it's understandable for everyone involved, including your Customer, as it will appear on all of your correspondence. From the example above, you notice that Kristy Abercrombie has 3 sub jobs, Family Room, Kitchen, and Remodel Bathroom.

When you develop sub jobs, all of your costs/credits will appear in the Balance Total for each particular sub job but will also flow up into the total for Kristy Abercrombie with a balance for all of her sub jobs.

Adding Sub Jobs

If you were to highlight Kristy Abercrombie, as in the example above, you have 3 options in order to add a sub job underneath the name.

Option 1 - use the drop-down menu and choose Add Job

Option 2 – Choose Edit from your Menu Bar, and then scroll down and choose Add Job

Option 3 – Click on Abercrombie, Kristy, and then right click on your mouse, and from there you will see a list of choices and choose Add Job will be the eighth one down.

When you add a new sub job, your customer information will appear with the resulting window above form. The Job Name section is highlighted, where you will enter the new Job Name. For this example, we will add a Sun Porch. You will notice in the example that the customer's information that has already been added will be automatically added to this new sub job.

The question about "How do I determine the opening balance?" refers to the total amount a customer owes in open invoices or statement charges as of the start date. This will be populated from entering any past open invoices.

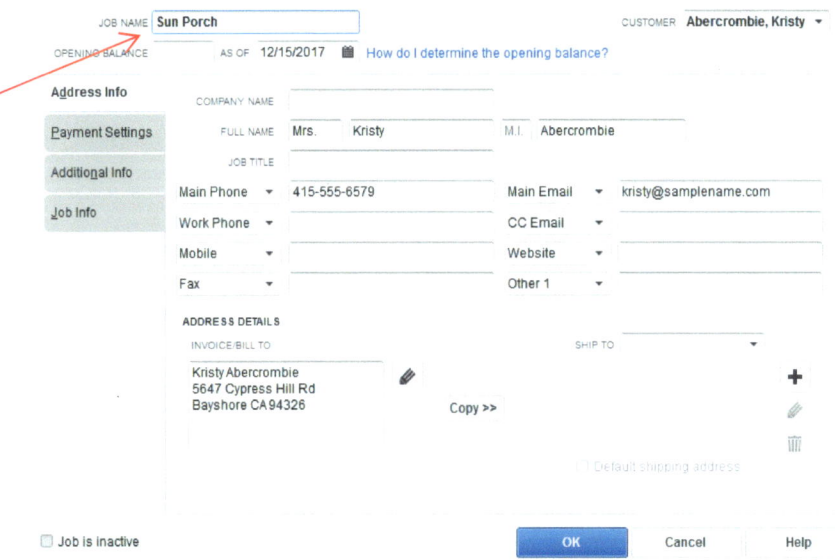

If you make a mistake by adding a job to the wrong customer, you have two options. The first option is that you can delete the job and retype it under the correct customer.

The second option you can go to the "Customer" field on the "Address Info" tab, use the drop down arrow to choose the correct customer, and then click the OK button. Unfortunately if you take the second option, all of the information from the initially wrong customer will still be present for that job and you must manually change it to the correct customer's information.

Job Info Tab

There's a fourth tab that appears called the Job Info Tab, which will carry the information you need for the job. This replaces the Sales Tax Settings tab in the Customer.

Job Description – you describe more specific information about the job itself

Job Type – you can use the drop down menu and choose the current default types (Extension, New Construction, Remodel, or Repairs), or you can add your own types by choosing the Add New button.

Job Status – you can use the drop down menu and choose the current default types (None, Pending, Awarded, In Progress, Closed, and Not Awarded). On this option, you cannot add any additional types.

Start Date – set this date for when you actually started the project

Projected End Date – set this date for when you are planning to end the project with your client

End Date – set this date for when you actually end the project with your client

*these options for start/projected end/end states are often used in the construction industry but you are not limited to use them in your business; it allows you the option to also measure your company's percentage of success in meeting deadlines and whether it's necessary to consider reviews for those projects for which the end dates are dramatically different than the projected end dates

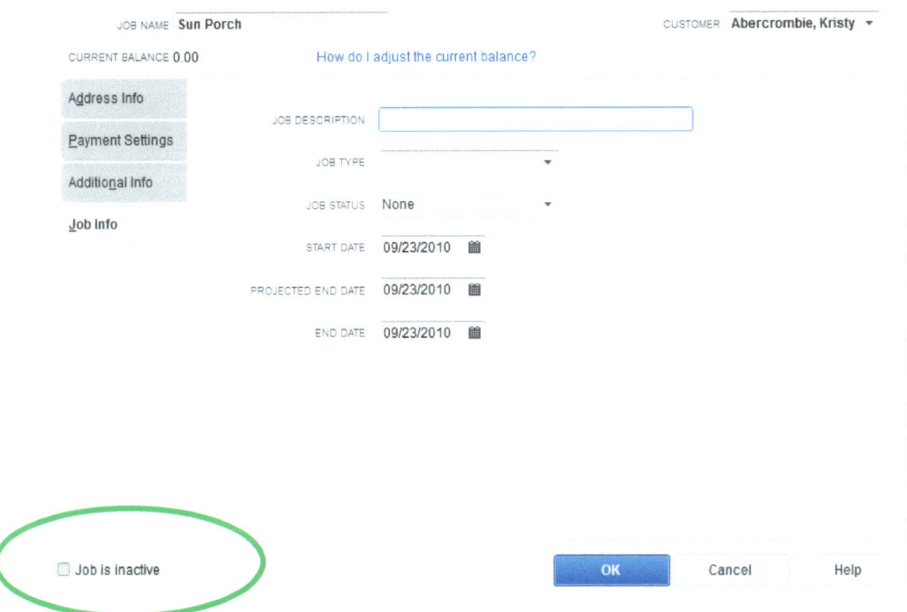

Inactive Customers & Jobs

When you are interested in no longer viewing a customer, vendor, employee, etc., you must remember that as long as they have a transaction associated with them, they cannot be deleted. This is the purpose of making them "Inactive." As you see in the green circle in the above example, if the box was checked next to "Job is inactive" you will see first-hand that the job is completed and no further transactions will be added to that job.

You can make your customer and/or job inactive by highlighting the item you're interested in, click on edit, check the box so it becomes inactive, and then clicking OK. When you return to the main Center screen, you no longer see the customer and/or job you made inactive. In this example, we are highlighting Sun Porch. Notice that you will see the title "Active Customers" from the drop-down menu above the Name section. This allows you to see only those customers that you still want to see and work with.

Before

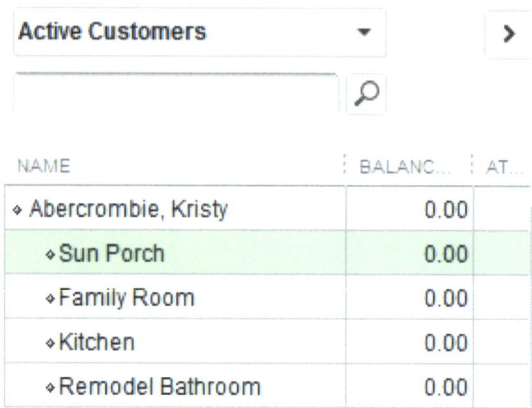

Check the Box

☑ Job is inactive

After

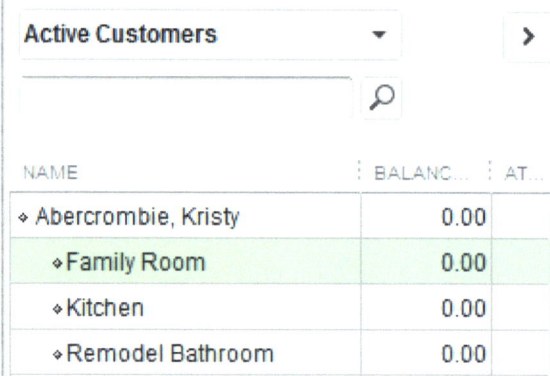

When you want to see all of the Customers and Jobs, you will then use your drop-down menu from the Active Customers and choose All Customers. You will see that the job Sun Porch is still there, even though it has been made inactive.

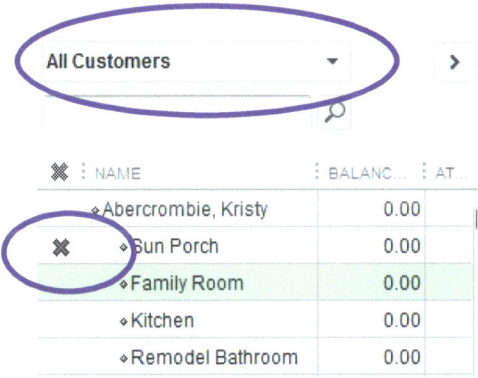

If you need to make the customer and/or job active again, go to the View box right under the Customers & Jobs tab, click the drop down arrow and choose All Customers. Afterwards you will see all of your inactive customers and/or jobs with an "X" beside their name. To make them active again, slide your cursor over the "X" until you see it turn also into an "X." When that happens, left click your mouse and it becomes active again. To show only your active customers and jobs now, go back to the View box drop down menu and click on Active Customers.

Customer Drop-Down Menu Options

Customers with Open Balances – show only those customers/jobs which allow you to see those which are active and have either receivables due you or credits due them

Customers with Overdue Invoices – show only those customers/jobs which allow you to see those who have surpassed their net terms without payment

Customers with Almost Due Invoices – show only those customers/jobs which allow you to see those who are nearing their net terms without payment

Custom Filter - allows you to search your Customer database for specific information in a variety of fields; the default is All common fields, but you can search through a variety of more specifics such as Name Fields, Address Fields, City, Zip Code, etc.

When you type in *Abercrombie*, into the "For" section, everything that has that name will appear in your search results. Because there is a comma after the name Abercrombie, that must also be added or you will not receive any results. To revert back to the Active Customers, click on the X next to Abercrombie.

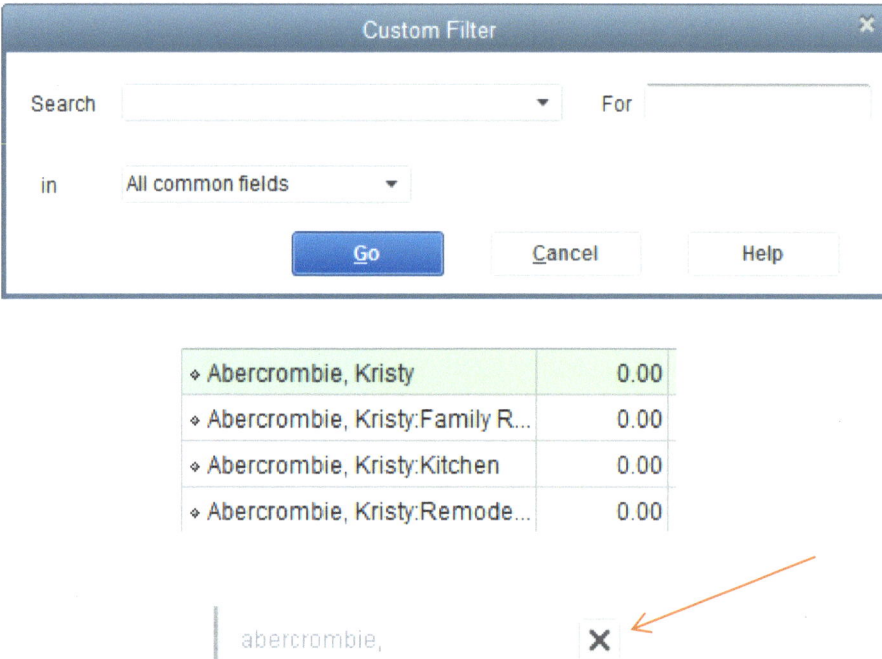

Another option in searching is through the blank box underneath your Active Customers drop-down menu. When you type in "Abercrombie," again, choose the magnifying glass (an icon you will see throughout QuickBooks), which will search for you and give you the same results.

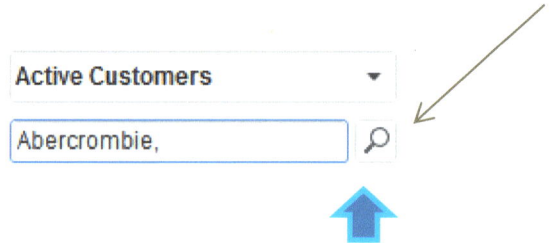

Exercises

1. If a Customer:Job is checked as inactive, you can no longer make it active again.

    a. True
    b. False

2. Determining the opening balance is a necessary component when creating jobs.

    a. True
    b. False

4. How many ways can you add a sub job?

    _____

5. If you add a sub job, then the transactions will be pulled into the

    _____.

5. What character is used to determine if a Customer is Inactive?

    a. W
    b. X
    c. Y
    d. Z

6. Set this date when you actually started the project refers to:

    a. Set Date
    b. Start Date
    c. Beginning Date

Objective 5 - Understanding the differences between: Estimate, Sales Order, Invoice, and Sales Receipt.

There are four main transactions between Customers, which are: Estimate, Sales Order, Invoice, and Sales Receipt.

Estimate

An estimate recorded in QuickBooks allows you to demonstrate to a Customer how much a particular project(s) and/or product(s) will initially cost based upon the parameters of their requirements. The Estimate DOES NOT affect the financial reporting, so there is financial obligation on behalf of the Customer until the actual Estimate is approved.

To create an Estimate, choose Customers from the Menu Bar, and then scroll down to the second option and choose Create Estimates. Each Estimate must have a Customer:Job chosen for it to be saved. If you use a general estimate for multiple customers, you can always set up a "dummy customer" to not retype the same information.

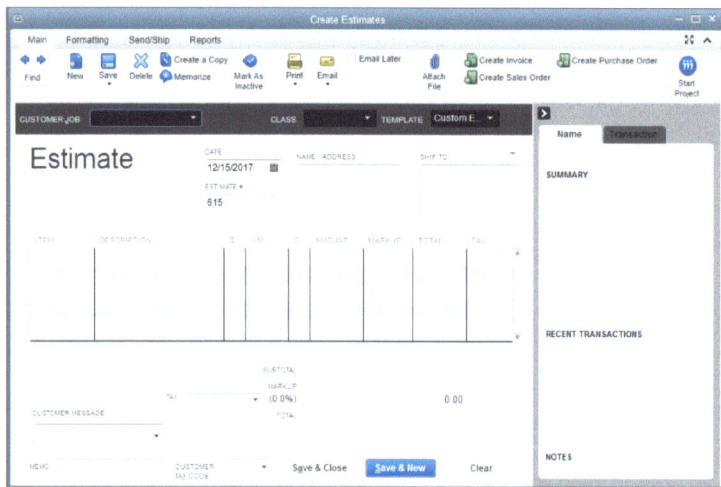

Sales Order

The Sales Order is often issued to the customer for products and/or services, which is an internal document of the company. The Sales order is created often upon receipt of a Customer's Purchase Order transaction for tracking purposes, so the Customer and you will be accurate in what is being purchased.

To Create a Sales Order, choose Customers from the Menu Bar, and then scroll down to the third option and choose Create Sales Order. Each Sales Order must have a Customer:Job chosen for it to be saved. If you use a general Sales Order for multiple customers, again you can always set up a "dummy customer" in order to not have to retype the same information each time.

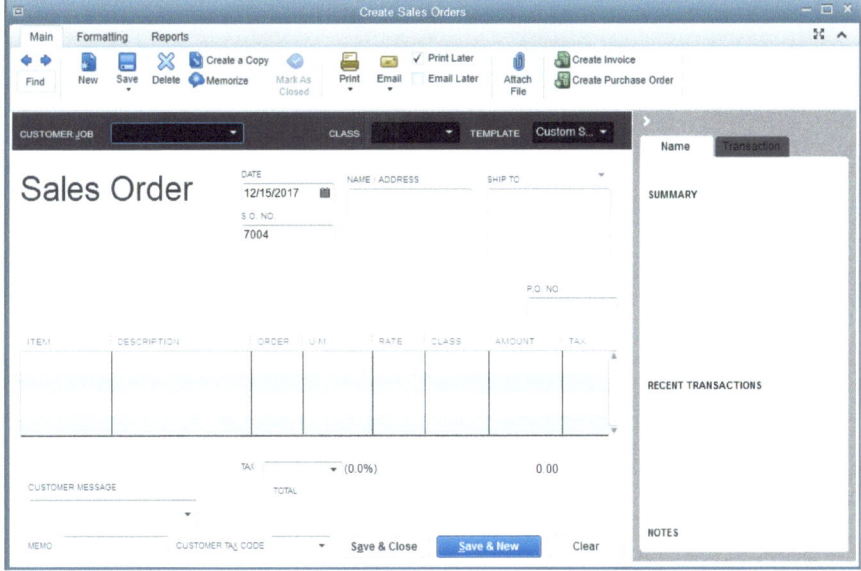

Invoice

The Invoice is issued to the customer for products and/or services, which there will be payment received at a later date.

To create an Invoice, choose Customers from the Menu Bar, and then scroll down to the fifth option and choose Create Invoices. Each Invoice must have a Customer:Job chosen for it to be saved. If you use a general Invoice for multiple customers, again you can always set up a "dummy customer" in order to not have to retype the same information each time. When an Invoice has been saved, it is applied to the Accounts Receivable account.

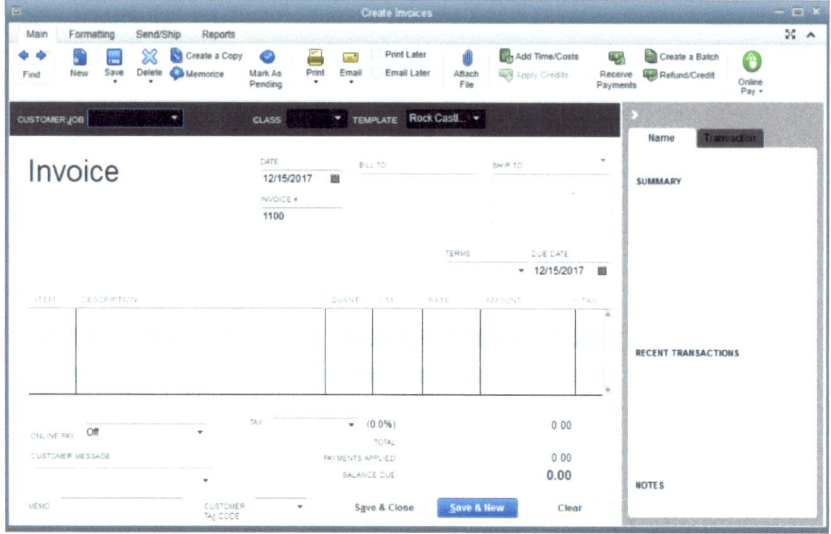

Sales Receipt

The Sales Receipt is issued to the customer for products and/or services, which payment is received at the time of the sale. To create a Sales Receipt, choose Customers from the Menu Bar, and then scroll down to the seventh option and choose Enter Sales Receipts. Each Sales Receipt DOES NOT require a Customer:Job for it to be saved.

If you use a general Sales Receipt for multiple customers, again you can always set up a "dummy customer" in order to not have to retype the same information each time. When a Sales Receipt has been saved, it is applied to either the bank account set-up or the Undeposited Funds account.

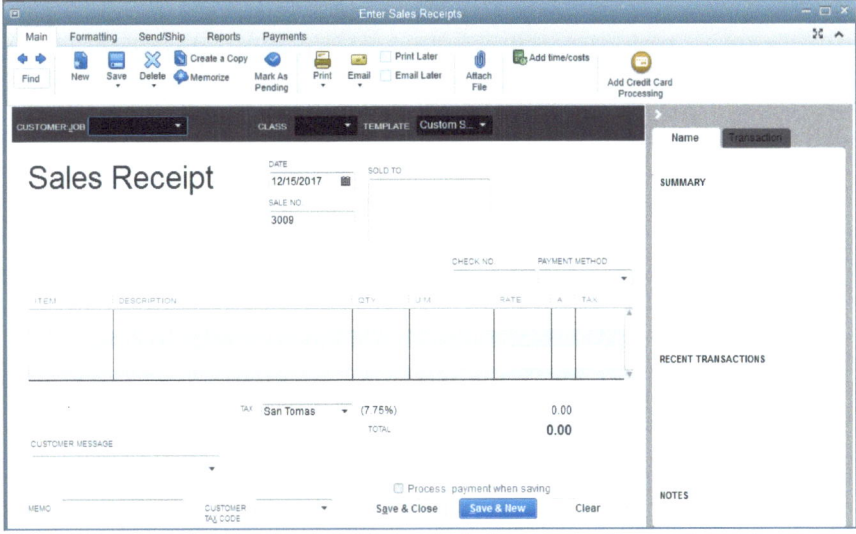

Exercises

1. A Sales Receipt directly affects a company's financial records.

    a. True
    b. False

2. When you create an Invoice, the amount is recorded into what account?

    a. Accounts Payable
    b. Accounts Receivable
    c. Checking Cccount
    d. Undeposited Funds Account

3. An Estimate directly affects a company's financial records.

    a. True
    b. False

4. A Sales Order directly affects a company's financial records.

    c. True
    d. False

5. The Sales Receipt requires a customer's contact information.

    a. True
    b. False

6. If you use a general estimate for multiple customers, you can always set up a "dummy customer" to not retype the same information.

    a. True
    b. False

Answer Key

Objective 1

1.	Ctrl-J	2.	Address Info
3.	False	4.	4
5.	True	6.	30
7.	False		

Objective 2

1. Excel
2. False

Objective 3

1.	False	2.	Voting Precinct
3.	False	4.	False
5.	buyer's sales tax permit #	6.	True
7.	True		

Objective 4

1.	False	2.	False
3.	three	4.	invoice
5.	X	6.	Beginning Date

Objective 5

1.	False	2.	Accounts Receivable
3.	False	4.	False
5.	False	6.	True